SOWING/GROWING/
KNOWING

CARL BEECH WITH
MARK GREENWOOD
IAN MANIFOLD

Carl

Carl is married to Karen and has two daughters. He's the leader of CVM (an international men's movement) and the founder of 'the code'. Previously a banker, church planter and senior pastor, he is convinced he is a great chef, plays the piano, loves cycling, movies and sci-fi books and caught a record-breaking catfish on the river Ebro in Spain.
Twitter @carlfbeech

Mark

Mark is married to Emma and has two girls. He is director of the 40:3 Trust and is dedicated to humorous, relevant and helpful communication. He loves curries, running, cycling, films and all things Apple. He is a Bradford City and Bradford Bulls fan. Formerly a butcher he's been in full time evangelism since 1988.
Twitter @ evangelistmark

Ian

Ian is a semi-retired cancer specialist who enjoys keeping fit, especially road cycling. He is married, with two daughters and five grandchildren. He runs an evangelistic Bible study group and is chairman of Christian Vision for Men.

Copyright © Carl Beech 2013
Published 2013 by CWR, Waverley Abbey House, Waverley Lane, Farnham,
Surrey GU9 8EP, UK.
Registered Charity No. 294387. Registered Limited Company No. 1990308.
The right of Carl Beech, Mark Greenwood and Ian Manifold to be identified as the
authors of this work has been asserted by them in accordance with the Copyright,
Designs and Patents Act 1988.

For a list of National Distributors visit www.cwr.org.uk/distributors
Unless otherwise indicated, all Scripture references are from the Holy Bible:
New International Version (NIV), copyright © 1973, 1978, 1984, 2011 by Biblica
(formerly the International Bible Society).
Other versions used: NLT: Scripture quotations marked NLT are taken from the Holy
Bible, New Living Translation, copyright © 1996, 2004, 2007 by Tyndale House
Foundation. Used by permission of Tyndale House Publishers, Inc., Carol Stream, Illinois
60188. All rights reserved.
Concept development, editing, design and production by CWR
Printed in Croatia by Zrinski
ISBN: 978-1-85345-944-3

Contents

[INTRO]

We've finally cracked it!
After being asked to write daily notes for men a number of times over the years, we've finally nailed it. So, in a nutshell, here you go and let the journey begin!

It's a simple and well-proven approach. The notes are between 200 and 300 words long. Each day begins with a verse and ends in a prayer. It will take you no more than a few minutes to read but I hope that what you read stays in your head throughout your day. The notes are numbered rather than dated, so it's OK if you miss a day to pick it back up. If you want to study with a group of guys you can easily keep track of where you are up to or swap ideas on that particular study online (we've a Facebook page). If you want to be part of a band of brothers internationally swapping thoughts, insights and prayer requests then you can do that as well by using our new Facebook page.

In each issue, I've asked some of my mates to contribute. In this one, big thanks to Mark Greenwood and Ian Manifold for their insights and thoughts. They're gunning for God and have some great things to say. We really hope that the subjects from Sowing to Growing speak into all our lives and help us stay on the narrow path.

So there it is. The Word of God has such power to inform and transform our lives, so let's knuckle down and get reading.

Your brother in Christ
Carl

[SAM THE MAN]

01/Chain reaction

'There was a certain man from Ramathaim, a Zuphite from the hill country of Ephraim, whose name was Elkanah son of Jeroham, the son of Elihu, the son of Tohu, the son of Zuph, an Ephraimite.'

1 Samuel 1:1

So, here we have Elkanah. I wonder if you've heard of him. (I suspect you won't have; but if you have, please accept my apologies and book me in for your next Bible knowledge tutorial!) Elkanah would regularly go and make a sacrifice to God and pray. He was a faithful man – and the legacy of his faithfulness was the great prophet Samuel. Elkanah's wife was Hannah and she was 'barren' – meaning she couldn't have children. God, however, responded to Elkanah's faithfulness, I believe, and, after He heard Hannah's prayer and her vow (see vv.9-11), she got pregnant and had a son.

And here is the moral of the story. You may think that God hasn't heard you. You may think that your faithfulness to Him has been overlooked and has gone unrewarded. You may think that your years of dedicated discipleship haven't borne any fruit. Without question, though, you would be mistaken. God has shown time and time again that He does hear the men and women who serve Him and He does reward their faithfulness. So, keep your head down and keep on keeping on! God sees it *all*.

Prayer: Father, thank You that You see and remember all I seek to do for You. Please keep my resolve strong to stay faithful to You. Amen.

02/ Promises, promises

'In her deep anguish Hannah prayed to the LORD, weeping bitterly. And she made a vow, saying, "LORD Almighty, if you will only look on your servant's misery and remember me, and not forget your servant but give her a son, then I will give him to the LORD for all the days of his life, and no razor will ever be used on his head."'

1 Samuel 1:10-11

Hannah kept her vow. She dedicated Samuel to the Lord, and in time he became a very powerful and influential prophet.

There's a story that goes like this. A man is stranded in the ocean after his boat sinks. Desperately, he prays: 'God, please save me from drowning. If You do, I'll give all my money to the poor!' A piece of wood large enough for him to sit on floats past, and he climbs onto it. He looks around at the sea stretching away on every side, and prays again: 'God, please make land appear. If You do, I'll serve You all my days!' A coastline suddenly appears on the horizon. He prays again: 'God, please make the current carry me in that direction. If You do, I will belong to You body and soul!' Finally, he is washed onto the shore. And he says a last quick prayer: 'Thanks, God. I won't forget this!'

He has effectively whittled his earlier promise to God down to nothing – and that is how we often behave. We call out to Him in our need and then, once He has answered our prayer, our commitment vanishes. Let's not be like the man in the water, let's be like the faithful Hannah, who delivered on her promises.

Prayer: I determine to be a man of my word. I will do as I promise and not be a man of empty rhetoric. Amen.

03/ It's a life thing

> "'So now I give him to the LORD. For his whole life he shall be given over to the LORD.' And he worshipped the LORD there.' **1 Samuel 1:28**

I love the commitment Hannah showed here. It's a bit of a problem that Samuel didn't get a say in the matter, of course, but that's an issue for another time. What grips me here is the sense of devotion, dedication and commitment to serve God wholeheartedly.

I guess that many men kind of treat their faith more like a hobby. Maybe that's true of you – I know I have been like this. It can still be a serious hobby, of course – but when the rubber hits the road and things get a bit painful, the hobby can easily take a back seat, thank you very much.

So, I'm thinking: Let's kick the hobby mentality into touch. Instead of listing our faith as one of our priorities – or even our top priority – let's place Jesus at the centre of all our activity and live a more integrated life. What we men tend to do is compartmentalise our lives. We have a work box, a family box, a church box, a sin box. And we close each box up when it doesn't suit us. Much better to merge all the boxes together, let the light into the areas of sin and live a life that is Jesus-centred! Let's give over our 'whole' lives, in the fullest sense of that word, to the Lord.

Prayer: I resolve to be a full-on man of faith, not a half-hearted, playing-at-it kind of guy. Help me to give my whole life over to You. Amen.

Commitment is an act, not a word.
JEAN-PAUL SARTRE

[MAN OF THE SPIRIT]

04/Bezalel

'Then the LORD said to Moses, "See, I have chosen Bezalel son of Uri, the son of Hur, of the tribe of Judah, and I have filled him with the Spirit of God, with wisdom, with understanding, with knowledge and with all kinds of skills – to make artistic designs for work in gold, silver and bronze, to cut and set stones, to work in wood, and to engage in all kinds of crafts. Moreover, I have appointed Oholiab son of Ahisamak, of the tribe of Dan, to help him. Also I have given ability to all the skilled workers to make everything I have commanded you.' **Exodus 31:1-6**

I've got a mate who can make anything out of anything. Seriously! He can look at a pile of old pallets and see a summer house. Then he builds it – and it rocks! I think that's an incredible gift, but one that is sadly underrated when it comes to spiritual matters. When people talk about spiritual gifts, they tend to think about things like healing, prophecy, tongues and visions. Rarely, however, is a gift for making stuff mentioned. I'm not sure why that is, because in my view – and, I believe, in the Bible's view – the Holy Spirit can 'anoint' (for want of a better term) practical things as well. That's certainly what Bezalel has going on here.

So, where am I going with this? It's simply that I think we need to have a more rounded view of how the Spirit works in our lives. Yes, there's the high-impact, supernatural stuff, but what about when God meets with us and equips us in the everyday? Perhaps we need more of a sense that when we fix something or come up with a solution to a practical problem, God is involved in that bit as well!

Prayer: Help me to see You in the ordinary and the practical as well as in the extraordinary and the supernatural. Amen.

05/Shadow man

'As a result, people brought those who were ill into the streets and laid them on beds and mats so that at least Peter's shadow might fall on some of them as he passed by.'

Acts 5:15

I've got a dog called Flick. She's a soppy German Shepherd who would be completely useless as a guard dog. And she gets an occasional fixation with shadows – she sees one and she jumps on it. That's about as close as I've ever come to an experience of something bizarre as far as shadows are concerned.

So, how do we make sense of this story? I think that what we have here is an extraordinary move of the Holy Spirit. Clearly, there is a huge surge of faith in the people and this is meeting with a very powerful anointing of the Spirit on Peter.

Now, we need to find a way to respond to this. Clearly, most of us are not going to have hordes of people throwing themselves into our shadow in the belief that it is carrying an overspill of God's healing power. All the same, I do think there is a challenge here for us to live with a greater expectation of God's presence. Are we ready to pray with people? Do we believe we will get a positive answer when we do? Are we walking closely with the Holy Spirit? Do we invite Him to be with us in our everyday encounters with people? All good questions to ask ourselves, I think.

Prayer: Make me a man of expectation. Help me to walk more closely with Your Spirit and to see Him at work in my everyday encounters with others. Amen.

06/Holy carrier pigeon?

'Paul and his companions travelled throughout the region of Phrygia and Galatia, having been kept by the Holy Spirit from preaching the word in the province of Asia.'
Acts 16:6

This is a fascinating little snippet of the Bible that raises all sorts of questions. I mean, how did the Holy Spirit stop Paul? Did He send a dream? A carrier pigeon? A bloke with a placard? Personally, I've come to realise that the Spirit talks to us in many different ways. Principally, of course, He talks to us through our regular reading of the Bible. Gradually, as we absorb the truth of its words, we start to see things more from God's perspective and instinctively to make more godly decisions. The verses we read become part of us and begin to inform our behaviour. But what of this more dramatic intervention?

I remember how a critical decision once had to be made in the church I was leading and we committed ourselves as a leadership to pray and fast over it. The night before the crucial meeting, I had a vivid dream – or more like a nightmare. It was some ten years ago but I can still recall the details to this day. I knew when I woke up that the Holy Spirit was warning us. I was amazed to find that all of my team had, by various routes, come to the same conclusion as me: that we needed to stop what we were doing. A month later, we discovered we had been spared from falling victim to a very serious fraud that could have hugely damaged the church.

We need to be sure to listen to the Holy Spirit – we ignore Him at our peril! He never contradicts the Bible but He does speak to us. Our job is to listen and act.

Prayer: Help me to be more attentive and responsive to the guidance of Your Spirit. Amen.

07/Good grief

'And do not grieve the Holy Spirit of God, with whom you were sealed for the day of redemption.'
Ephesians 4:30

Let me pass on something I've learned about the Holy Spirit. Take this on board and it could revolutionise your walk with God. He's really sensitive to our character and conduct.

'Grieve' the Holy Spirit and (to use the image of a dove) He may just flutter away from you. I'm not saying that God abandons us when we sin but rather that we diminish the power and presence of His Spirit in our lives. More frightening still is the fact that often we don't even realise that we've caused Him to leave us. Samson is a case in point – towards the end of his life, we are told (Judg. 16:20), God's presence left him and he didn't even know! You may be wondering how on earth something like that can happen. It comes about because you numb and blunt your conscience over a long period of time.

You take a wrong turning and don't correct your mistake. You sin and don't confess it. The law of diminishing returns applies and so you keep pushing the limits of what is acceptable, until finally you have removed yourself so far away from God that you're a shadow of the man you once were. It's subtle and deadly but it happens to all too many fellas out there.

So, here's the deal. Surround yourself with good people. Examine yourself and your heart often and don't hesitate to correct yourself. Keep short accounts with God and deal with creeping sin quickly and decisively.

Prayer: Keep me vigilant and honest about where I am in my walk with You. Stop me in my tracks if I'm blunting Your presence. Amen.

08/No brawling

'Get rid of all bitterness, rage and anger, brawling and slander, along with every form of malice.'
Ephesians 4:31

On the subject of grieving the Holy Spirit, here are some pithy pointers as to the kind of thing we indulge in that should set off an alarm bell in our heads and hearts. Dealing with brawling is pretty obvious, really – just don't do it! Avoid the punch-ups at the pub and all will be well. But what about the others?

Someone once said that being bitter is like letting someone live in your head rent-free. It's true. Nothing good ever comes from it – it only takes you to dark places. Oftentimes, harbouring bitterness leads to 'rage and anger'. Sure, there are other things that will take you there, too, but let's just say for now that if you keep your head in a negative place about people and about stuff that is happening around you, it's most likely that you will end up being one angry bloke!

Overload with that kind of emotion and at some point you will end up losing it – and that's called 'rage'. Slander, too – which means badmouthing other people – is an outworking of bitterness, insecurity and jealousy.

It takes discipline to keep on the right side of those bad boys. In the words of an old friend of mine: 'Sometimes we just need to wind our necks in'.

Prayer: When the bitterness is building up and I can feel myself giving in to rage, remind me to get a grip and pursue the path of peace. Amen.

[FRUIT LOOP]

09/Not nice

'But the fruit of the Spirit is love,
joy, peace, forbearance, kindness,
goodness, faithfulness, gentleness
and self-control. Against such
things there is no law. Those
who belong to Christ Jesus have
crucified the flesh with its passions
and desires. Since we live by the
Spirit, let us keep in step with the
Spirit. Let us not become conceited,
provoking and envying each other.'
Galatians 5:22-26

We'll be looking at this chunk of the Bible for
the next few days, and I want to start by nailing
a particular myth I find pretty disabling. For
some reason, followers of Jesus have for far
too long misunderstood these verses to mean
being sugary-sweet and nice. I don't think that
was ever meant to be the case. Nice is bland and
doesn't get us very far. I remember hearing a
NASA engineer talking some months after the
second shuttle disaster. He said something like

this: 'We lost the ability to be ruthlessly honest because we were more concerned about being nice to each other.' In other words, they had been unable to be critical and analytical about what they were doing.

I see this in the church, too. We are so anxious to be nice that we don't always call something what it is. Love can be painful because it's honest. Being patient can hurt as we journey with people and struggle through conflict. Being kind to our enemies can be exhausting, and being gentle in response to anger takes real guts. More than that, confronting wrongdoing can be an expression of love when we are protecting those around us. I hope you see what I'm getting at. The qualities Paul lists here can be tough, if we understand them the way I think we are meant to.

Prayer: Help me to love till it hurts, to exercise patience even when it drains me, and to be kind to my enemies. Amen.

10/Kindness

> 'But the fruit of the Spirit is love, joy, peace, forbearance, kindness, goodness, faithfulness, gentleness and self-control. Against such things there is no law. Those who belong to Christ Jesus have crucified the flesh with its passions and desires. Since we live by the Spirit, let us keep in step with the Spirit. Let us not become conceited, provoking and envying each other.'
> **Galatians 5:22-26**

What does it mean to be kind? Helping an old lady across the road? Making a round of drinks in the office when it isn't your turn? Paying someone a compliment? All of these things and more are kind – but is there a more radical interpretation?

What about taking a friend to one side and, out of concern for them, pointing out a blind spot? What about standing in the gap between two warring parties, taking a hit if necessary?

What about taking the blame for something to protect someone else who's more vulnerable than you? Surely, these actions are kind, too? So, why don't we see them as such? Kindness doesn't have to look like something out of a Disney film. It can be tough, uncompromising and gritty. It can take us into painful places and cost us dearly.

So, let's start manning up the fruit of the Spirit. Let's look for opportunities to exercise our God-given strength and demonstrate a radical kindness that shakes things up and puts things right. That's far more exciting than carrying someone's shopping for them – not that we shouldn't still do that, of course!

Prayer: As I look for opportunities to be radically kind, strengthen my resolve and give me the guts to do the painful things, not just the sugary-sweet stuff. Amen.

11/Keep a lid on it

'But the fruit of the Spirit is love, joy, peace, forbearance, kindness, goodness, faithfulness, gentleness and self-control. Against such things there is no law. Those who belong to Christ Jesus have crucified the flesh with its passions and desires. Since we live by the Spirit, let us keep in step with the Spirit. Let us not become conceited, provoking and envying each other.' **Galatians 5:22-26**

Let's think about patience. Every day brings a moment when you need to exercise some. It could be when you're running late for a meeting and you're stuck in a traffic jam, or the customer in front of you is hogging the sales assistant's time. Or perhaps a call centre is keeping you endlessly on hold ... Any situation like that calls for us to exercise a degree of self-discipline. I think it's a key requirement for us men of God to keep our heads, not least so that we maintain a good witness in front of other people.

There is, however, a more radical patience. What about caring for someone who has significant medical or emotional needs? What about continuing to love someone for years when they only give you a hard time? That is long-haul patience and it takes things to a different level! Both kinds of patience may oblige us to grit our teeth, but this kind requires us to dig into our emotional reserves as well.

The question is: how do you become a master of patience? I think it boils down to prayer and chill-out time. Pray through the trials and tribulations and find time to relax if you possibly can – that's a winning combination. Be kind to yourself and don't beat yourself up. Do stuff that makes you laugh and avoid getting all intense about stuff that doesn't really matter in the grand scheme of things. You'll have deeper emotional reserves as a result and more to give.

Prayer: Help me to keep my inner peace and not to lose it when I'm up against it, both today and in the long haul. Amen.

12/ Goody two-shoes

'But the fruit of the Spirit is love, joy, peace, forbearance, kindness, goodness, faithfulness, gentleness and self-control. Against such things there is no law. Those who belong to Christ Jesus have crucified the flesh with its passions and desires. Since we live by the Spirit, let us keep in step with the Spirit. Let us not become conceited, provoking and envying each other.'
Galatians 5:22-26

Goodness is an interesting concept for us to think about. As a bloke, I can easily go into warrior mode – I can feel the forces at work inside me that make me want to go to war when someone has been wronged (and especially me!). It seems to me, however, that the very essence of goodness is to do pretty much the opposite. True goodness isn't all about dashing around doing 'good deeds'; it's to do with spine and heart.

And that means that we need to get into long-term character development. We need to train ourselves so that our instinctive reaction is always to believe the best of someone and give them the benefit of the doubt. And the only way to achieve that, really, is to be prepared to take a hit sometimes. We may well show trust in someone, or do good to them, only for it to backfire and get thrown back in our faces. So be it. That's life. We just have to crack on – and put a stop to any negative thoughts before they have a chance to worm their way into our hearts.

Prayer: Keep my thoughts and actions pure and free from cynicism and all that is far from good. Amen.

13/Man of peace

'But the fruit of the Spirit is love, joy, peace, forbearance, kindness, goodness, faithfulness, gentleness and self-control. Against such things there is no law. Those who belong to Christ Jesus have crucified the flesh with its passions and desires. Since we live by the Spirit, let us keep in step with the Spirit. Let us not become conceited, provoking and envying each other.'
Galatians 5:22-26

What does it mean to be a man of peace? Jesus talked about us being peacemakers in the Sermon on the Mount and said that those who play that role will be called 'children of God' (Matt. 5:9). Again, I suspect we've seen an unfortunate slide into a pretty bland understanding of what this means. Being a man of peace isn't about looking all contented in a field full of fluffy animals. A true man of peace is prepared to put himself in harm's way. He stands in the breach on behalf of someone weaker. He brokers peace even if it means taking a hit himself. A true peacemaker can and will get bruised in the pursuit of his objective.

A classic example might be Gandhi, who was one of the pioneers of non-violent resistance (inspired, I believe, by the teaching and example of Jesus). He really lived out what it means to turn the other cheek and take a beating. So powerful was his peacemaking that Lord Mountbatten described him as a 'one-man peace army'. Be prepared today to stand in the breach. Be prepared to take a hit. Forget self-preservation and be a real man of peace!

Prayer: Give me the guts to do what is right and take a hit on behalf of peace. Amen.

[BATTLE FIT]

14/ Body and soul

'Dear friend, I pray that you may enjoy good health and that all may go well with you, just as you are progressing spiritually.' **3 John 2**

Some time ago, I heard about a guy in some church who had what was being described as a miraculous recovery from a heart attack. Nice one! There's nothing like a good story about God's intervention in a situation to build our faith and inspire us. On this occasion, however, they were telling only half the story. The bloke concerned was huge. I mean, he was seriously overweight and out of shape. It's great that he recovered and everything, but to be honest he was a heart attack waiting to happen.

One of my mates is a GP and he tells me that, as far as he can see, Christian men are dying before their time because they are packing the food away and not getting up off the sofa. I felt very convicted about this a few years ago and so I've made sure ever since that I get regular exercise and also do an annual fitness challenge of some kind.

So, I love the holistic angle of this verse. It's like: 'Yeah, I really hope you're walking with God, but I hope your body is in good shape, too'. As men who follow Jesus, I think we have a responsibility here to honour the bodies God has given us (whatever our genetics) and do what we can to keep them in the best shape possible.

Prayer: Father, help me to be a role model by being healthy in every respect – not just spiritually but physically as well. Amen.

Take care of your body. It's the only place you have to live.
JIM ROHN

15/Prize possession

'Do you not know that your bodies are temples of the Holy Spirit, who is in you, whom you have received from God? You are not your own; you were bought at a price. Therefore honour God with your bodies.' **1 Corinthians 6:19-20**

I love the strength of these verses. Plain and to the point – they say it like it is. The fact is, you don't belong to yourself. As a follower of Jesus, you now belong to Him. You may think you are master of your own life, but while it's true that we are free (to an extent) to make certain choices about the way we live, that is only because of God's grace. We have no rights. We are now Christ's bondservants – His slaves.

And His requirements are clear: we are to keep our bodies healthy and fit. Partly because that is the right thing to do anyway, but also because living sensibly makes us better able to serve Him with all our strength and ability. Until such time as Jesus calls us home, we should be doing our bit to stand firm on the front lines of the battle of faith. We were bought at a price, so we should live well in response to that. I meet far too many Christian men who shovel too much food and too much booze down their necks. I believe we need to challenge this culture. I'm not asking you to go over the top and get all puritanical about it. Rather, I'm saying: Let's take these verses seriously and look after our bodies. Watch the booze intake, take some gentle exercise, don't shovel in too much lard. Let's be an example to those around us. Simple, really.

Prayer: Help me to take these verses seriously and take some action in response. Help me to keep my body fit and free from addiction. Amen.

16/ Spiritual fitness

'For physical training is of some value, but godliness has value for all things, holding promise for both the present life and the life to come.'
1 Timothy 4:8

Let's think today about not just physical fitness but spiritual fitness as well. What does it mean to be godly? It can't mean just that we go to church, give some money, sing some songs and help in the kids' work. Much as all these things have value, there must be more to it than that! I think the clue is in the second part of this verse. Godly people have their eyes fixed on Jesus in the present but also live with a sense of their destiny. They have put their hope in Jesus so profoundly that it has a visible effect on them.

You can't get to that place overnight, of course. Verse 7 in the same chapter tells us we need to train ourselves to be godly. When you're preparing for a marathon, you can't go out and run 26.2 miles straight off – you have to build up to it over many months. (I know, I've done it!) It takes discipline to stick to the programme and keep going out in bad weather. Training for godliness is very similar. It's a discipline to remain in the Word of God every day, and a discipline to commit time to pray and listen to God. It takes even more discipline then to live it out!

So, get serious about this. Make prayer lists and put 'em all over your house. Memorise chunks of the Bible. Commit to make some sacrifices. Start building up the miles and before you know it, you'll have covered more ground with God than you'd believed was possible. I've learned that the more seriously you take living out your faith, the more seriously God will take you and the more He will trust you with.

Prayer: I commit to getting into serious training to get spiritually fit. Help me make the right decisions and stick to them. Amen.

[A FAST BLAST THROUGH JOHN]

17/Stay radical

'The next day John was there again with two of his disciples. When he saw Jesus passing by, he said, "Look, the Lamb of God!" When the two disciples heard him say this, they followed Jesus. Turning round, Jesus saw them following and asked, "What do you want?" They said, "Rabbi" (which means "Teacher"), "where are you staying?"'
John 1:35-38

I love this – it's an awesome picture of radical 'followship'. John the Baptist recognises Jesus for who He is and when he declares it out loud, his two disciples start to follow Jesus. Literally. It's an amazing story of a couple of guys who are so overcome by who Jesus is, and so committed to pursuing the truth, they literally take off after Him.

When I first met Jesus, I kind of felt the same way. It was a game-changing moment for an 18-year-old guy – I dropped all my plans and ambitions to follow Him. Even in my twenties I had quite a radical sense of what it meant to be a disciple. I left my job and worked unpaid as a student pastor. I spent all my savings on putting myself through Bible college. I moved onto an estate so I could plant a church. I committed what some people called 'financial suicide'. To me, though, it didn't matter. I'd met Jesus and that was all that mattered.

As time goes by, however, it becomes a challenge to remain that radical – but I believe we must. We have no other option, in my opinion. We may not quit our jobs – there's no evidence, after all, that all the disciples left their livelihoods behind – but let's stay sharp in walking close to Jesus and keeping our eyes on Him. Let's keep that sense of awe we felt when we first met Him – or pray that we recover it.

Prayer: I desire to be a man who walks in Your footsteps. I will follow You with all my heart, soul, mind and strength. Amen.

18/Trashing the Temple

'When it was almost time for the Jewish Passover, Jesus went up to Jerusalem. In the temple courts he found people selling cattle, sheep and doves, and others sitting at tables exchanging money. So he made a whip out of cords, and drove all from the temple courts, both sheep and cattle; he scattered the coins of the money-changers and overturned their tables. To those who sold doves he said, "Get these out of here! Stop turning my Father's house into a market!"'

John 2:13-16

Jesus gets angry here at something quite particular: traders were taking advantage of the gathering of people for the Passover to make a fast buck. So, He takes action. This isn't a picture of Jesus 'meek and mild'. This is Him full of righteous indignation and demanding a response.

So, my question to you is this: What is your temple scenario and what action are you taking about it? I really do believe it's entirely right for us to get angry about some things. In fact, I think that sanctified anger is an entirely appropriate response. Hope believes that things can change and become better than they are. Sometimes, however, in order for that to happen, people need to take action.

So, what is it that gets your goat? What injustice makes you so indignant that you really wish you could do something about it? Jesus made Himself a whip and upended some tables. Maybe you could harness your testosterone and throw yourself into making a difference over some local issue? I'm throwing out a challenge. Use your strength to defend the weak and the needy, stand up for what is right and make the presence of God's kingdom felt!

Prayer: Lord, take my frustration and sense of injustice and use them for Your purposes. Amen.

19/New start, new hope

'Jesus replied, "Very truly I tell you, no one can see the kingdom of God unless they are born again."' `John 3:3`

When I was a teenager, 'born again' meant one thing and one thing only: Cliff Richard. He released the song *Mistletoe and Wine* in 1988 when I was 16 and let's just say it wasn't our first choice of listening material. Most of us thought he was somewhat cheesy – just another 'born-again' Christian releasing rubbish. The problem was, it made the phrase 'born again' feel really cheesy, too.

That all changed on 22 April 1990 at around 7pm, when I met Jesus.

Walking out of the church 45 minutes later, I felt like the world was a new place. It was like I had stepped out of a scratchy black-and-white picture into a multicoloured HD one. It was astonishing. Being born again means a fresh start. It means you have taken a decision to walk away from your old life to begin a new one with Jesus as your Lord. For me, it meant handing over to Him all the plans I had for my life – for Him to use, lose or adapt as He saw fit.

I've learned over the years since then that being born again is actually a continuing conscious decision for us. We need to keep coming back to the kind of mindset we had when we took our first steps towards the kingdom. Otherwise, we're in danger of losing focus and straying off what Jesus called 'the narrow road' (Matt. 7:14). Why don't you take a pause today and commit your plans, and hopes and dreams, to Him? Give them to Him to use, lose or adapt. Make today another fresh start, and crack on with the journey!

Prayer: Thank You, Lord, that You rescued me and gave me a new life. Now take that life and use it for Your glory. Amen.

20/Storm force

'A strong wind was blowing and the waters grew rough. When they had rowed about three or four miles, they saw Jesus approaching the boat, walking on the water; and they were frightened. But he said to them, "It is I; don't be afraid."'

John 6:18-20

Many years ago, I was up against it a bit with some serious issues that needed confronting in an organisation I led. I can remember it all vividly, even though it was over ten years ago. The night before the real crunch meeting, I barely slept a wink. Every time I thought through the various possible outcomes, my heart would begin to race. Not good.

The time came to head off to the meeting and I will never forget what happened next. My wife, Karen, gave me a kiss on the cheek and said: 'With Jesus in the vessel, you can smile at the storm.' I said: 'What?' 'It's an old song we used to sing in Sunday school,' she told me, and she sang the whole thing to me on the front steps of our house.

I'll tell you what, I couldn't believe the effect it had on me. As I sat in that meeting humming the tune, I felt an incredible sense of peace wash over me. It was the presence of the Holy Spirit, breathing calm into the situation and reminding me of the reality of what we have when we know Jesus. That truth can be an incredible comfort even in the midst of the fiercest storm.

Prayer: When the chips are down and the storm is raging around me, remind me of Your presence with me. Amen.

There are some things you learn best in calm, and some in storm.
WILLA CATHER

[LIVING LIFE ON THE UP]

21/Wise up to weakness

'Humble yourselves, therefore, under God's mighty hand, that he may lift you up in due time.' **1 Peter 5:6**

Three ministers were in an accountability group and meeting for the first time. They agreed to be honest with each other from the word go. 'I have a problem of violence towards my church members,' the first one said. 'I have a problem with stealing from church funds,' said the second. The third minister said: 'I have a problem with gossip and can't wait till we finish.'

This verse is interesting. It doesn't just tell us to be humble, it's stronger than that – 'Humble *yourselves*' (my emphasis). Have you noticed that we're humble until somebody points out our faults or weaknesses and then we aren't so humble after all? Humility is the ability to see ourselves as God sees us. My experience – my frustration – is that it's often only when I'm tempted that I discover who I really am. I wonder how well we really know ourselves.

One of my weaknesses is materialism. The minute I got my iPhone 4S, I was waiting to get the 5. If I actually had any money, I would be disastrous! The truth is, our weaknesses can be weaknesses even if we don't get the opportunity to give in to them. The fact that I don't have the money to buy an iPhone 5 or my dream car, a Range Rover, doesn't actually mean that my materialistic desires aren't a weakness.

If I want to live life on the up, I need to wise up to weakness. You know what it's like when you offer someone help but because they don't think they need it – they're *fine* – it's impossible to give it? The reason we need to humble ourselves is so that we don't make it impossible for God to help us and lift us up.

Prayer: What are my weaknesses? Help me, Lord, to humble myself enough to accept that I have them. Help me to know myself as you know me. Amen.

22/Give up what feeds it

'Be alert and of sober mind. Your enemy the devil prowls around like a roaring lion looking for someone to devour.' **1 Peter 5:8**

A preacher decided that a visual aid would demonstrate that not everything is good for us. Four worms were placed in separate jars. The first contained alcohol, the second contained cigarette smoke, the third contained chocolate syrup and the fourth contained good, clean soil. At the end of his sermon, the preacher reported the following results: the worm in the alcohol was dead, the worm in the cigarette smoke was dead, the worm in the chocolate syrup was dead but the worm in the good, clean soil was still alive. He asked the congregation what they learned about life from this demonstration. Dave shouted out: 'As long as you drink, smoke and eat chocolate, you won't have worms!'

We need to know what is good for us and not just what is not bad for us. We are encouraged in this verse to do two things: be alert *and* be of sober mind. It makes sense to be alert because the devil does know what our weaknesses are. The interesting thing about the phrase 'be of sober mind' is that literally it means 'be self-controlled and sensible'. Sometimes as Christians we aren't very sensible in the way we live our lives. There is a fine line between faith and folly and I know I don't always get it right.

I do believe in prayer and God's protection but I wonder if sometimes we just need to be a bit more sensible. To make a really successful temptation takes two people – and you're one of them! Don't go past a greasy cafe if you're trying to diet. We need to wise up to weakness and then give up what feeds it.

Prayer: What are the things I do that are just not sensible, that constantly keep me weak? Help me, Lord, to stop feeding my weaknesses. Amen.

23/ Get up and fight it

'Resist him, standing firm in the faith, because you know that the family of believers throughout the world is undergoing the same kind of sufferings.' **1 Peter 5:9**

Here's a true story. A schoolteacher injured his back and had to wear a plaster cast round the upper part of his body. It fitted under his shirt and wasn't noticeable at all. On the first day of term, he found himself assigned to the toughest class in the school. Walking confidently into their rowdy classroom, he opened the window as wide as possible and then busied himself with some work. When a sudden breeze made his tie flap, he took the desk stapler and stapled his tie (so it seemed) to his chest. He had no problem with discipline that term.

This verse tells us to resist and stand firm. One problem with this, of course, is that we can get caught up in these words and not consider their context. We can often put all our effort into resisting and standing firm without putting into place some simple principles that will help us.

I remember being in a tug-of-war contest once (which my team won, of course). We were told to 'take the strain' before we were told to pull. I want to encourage you to take the strain *before* you try to resist and stand firm. The previous two entries give us the context, and therefore the knowledge of how we can resist. Let me sum it up like this: first, wise up to your weakness and, second, give up what feeds it. This will put us on a good footing to 'resist' and 'stand firm'.

Prayer: Help me to live my life on a good footing. Give me the confidence to get up and fight rather than feeling defeated. Amen.

24/Look up and expect

'And the God of all grace, who called you to his eternal glory in Christ, after you have suffered a little while, will himself restore you and make you strong, firm and steadfast.' **1 Peter 5:10**

A few years ago, I received an amusing email telling me how to annoy people. It included such suggestions as: Speak only in a robot voice; start each meal by conspicuously licking your food 'so that no one can steal it'; sniffle incessantly; walk a few steps behind someone spraying everything they touch with antibacterial spray; and, finally, leave your indicator on for 50 miles while driving in the middle lane of a motorway. I love it! I wonder what you could add to the list.

In this verse, Peter gives us both encouragement and a dose of reality. God will bring us through, he says, but only after we have suffered a little while. I'm not sure whether to take comfort from this or not. The truth is, there are lots of things that will irritate and frustrate us – not least, other people! There will be temptations and trials that get the better of us and set us back. And yet I do believe, from what the Bible says as well as from my own experience – and maybe you can say the same – that with more vigilance we will see more victories. Temptations and trials are everywhere, but you know what? So is the grace of God!

So, let me encourage you to wise up to weakness, give up what feeds it, get up and fight it and, finally, look up and expect it. Expect that it will happen, but look up to God!

Prayer: Help me to do all I can to 'live life on the up' – but, when I fail, to know more of Your love, Your grace and Your forgiveness. Amen.

25/Maglight

'When Jesus spoke again to the people, he said, "I am the light of the world. Whoever follows me will never walk in darkness, but will have the light of life."' **John 8:12**

I remember reading about a fascinating time in church history when Martin Luther, a reformer, was due to appear in front of a kind of church court that could have had him put to death. Story has it that he cried out to God all through the night before the hearing – but felt absolutely nothing. Undeterred, he appeared before the court the next day and, after standing firm against the charges laid against him, he finished by saying this: 'I stand convicted' – that is, convinced – 'by the Scriptures to which I have appealed, and my conscience is taken captive by God's word. I cannot and will not recant anything, for to act against our conscience is neither safe for us, nor open to us.'

In his darkest hour, he clung to the truth as he saw it. He didn't rely on his feelings, and a nice warm sensation that God was with him, but on his conscience. I like that. It speaks of a man who knew that the Holy Spirit was within him. His circumstances may have been dark but that didn't dictate his response. I think that's a realistic understanding of what it means to 'walk in the light'. *Know* it, because you won't always *feel* it. So, take this verse to heart in all you are doing and know that what Jesus says is true, no matter what you feel.

Prayer: Thank You that in Jesus I walk in the light and will never be in darkness, no matter what my circumstances are. Amen.

26/It's emotional

'Jesus, once more deeply moved, came to the tomb. It was a cave with a stone laid across the entrance. "Take away the stone," he said. "But, Lord," said Martha, the sister of the dead man, "by this time there is a bad odour, for he has been there four days." Then Jesus said, "Did I not tell you that if you believe, you will see the glory of God?" So they took away the stone. Then Jesus looked up and said, "Father, I thank you that you have heard me. I knew that you always hear me, but I said this for the benefit of the people standing here, that they may believe that you sent me." When he had said this, Jesus called in a loud voice, "Lazarus, come out!"' **John 11:38-43**

This is a profound and dramatic miracle, no question. I flippin' love the direct command of

Jesus – it's almost like He is taking on all the forces of nature that have ended Lazarus' life. He stands in the breach and goes to battle. Awesome! However, the bit of the story that leaps out at me is the detail in verse 38: Jesus is deeply moved. His stand against the power of death here is motivated by His compassion for Lazarus and for those who are grieving for him.

So often I feel that is missing in us guys. Ask yourself when was the last time you felt so moved that you would stake everything on taking action. I remember one bloke being so stirred by the plight of some people in the Far East that he set up a charity to help them. Until then his faith had been a bit lukewarm, but suddenly, as he did his bit to change the world, it came alive. Compassion is a powerful force. Ask God to stir your heart to action today!

Prayer: Make me a man who is prepared to stand in the breach to see Your kingdom come. Amen.

27/Get in there

'I will remain in the world no longer, but they are still in the world, and I am coming to you. Holy Father, protect them by the power of your name, the name you gave me, so that they may be one as we are one. ... My prayer is not that you take them out of the world but that you protect them from the evil one.'
John 17:11,15

All too often, believers can develop something akin to a siege mentality. We bunker down with a kind of survivalist attitude – we even sing songs in church that say 'How long till You come and rescue us?'. It's interesting, then, that Jesus doesn't actually pray here that we will be taken out of the world, but rather that we will be one and will be protected. We'll talk about unity tomorrow, but for now let's focus on the idea that Jesus actually wants us here, getting stuck in with some kingdom living.

Understanding that Jesus wants us to get stuck in has been a game-changer for me. It spurs me to action. We're not just trying to get through life until the day He calls us home, we're trying to get our hands dirty and make a difference. And that means we need protection. Why? Because there's a war on. Our job is to get stuck into it and fight. To seize opportunities to bear witness to Jesus. To make the presence of God's kingdom felt. To pray and engage with issues of injustice. To use our time and talents to do our bit where we are. The enemy won't like that and that's why Jesus prays that we will be protected by the power of His name. So, make the most of the life you've been given and get stuck in!

Prayer: I won't hide from the world but will engage with it, using all I have to make the presence of Your kingdom felt. Amen.

28/United we stand

'My prayer is not for them alone. I pray also for those who will believe in me through their message, that all of them may be one, Father, just as you are in me and I am in you. May they also be in us so that the world may believe that you have sent me.' **John 17:20-21**

It's an old story but I'll tell you what, I have genuinely heard people say that they don't believe in the God of the Bible because the churches all seem to disagree with each other. Sad, isn't it? In fact, I've actually been present in churches where there have been rows over the coffee, the squash cupboard, the car parking and – wait for it! – the colour of the walls. How pathetic!

I strongly believe that we need to fight for unity. So much is at stake. If Jesus made it a core theme of the longest prayer by Him that we have on record, it's got to be important, right? Disunity can be caused by many things: envy, insecurity, small-mindedness and majoring on minor things ... I often say to the guys who work for me at CVM: 'Don't take yourselves too seriously, but take the mission seriously. Don't get wound up by insignificant things, only get wound up by the fact that not enough people are becoming followers of Jesus.'

In other words, let's keep it real and all try to stay on the same page as each other!

Prayer: I resolve not to let insignificant things harm my relationships. I will strive for unity in the Church so that I honour You, Jesus. Amen.

29/Doing life together

'They devoted themselves to the apostles' teaching and to fellowship, to the breaking of bread and to prayer.' **Acts 2:42**

So, the other day it got to 6pm and I was pretty much done in. I'd got up early and had dashed from meeting to meeting all day – and, to add to the pressure, I was a tad behind in my writing schedule for these daily notes. (Well, maybe more than a tad behind, if I'm honest ...) In other words, I was under pressure. I got home at 6.30pm only to remember that we had a home group at 7pm. Every bone in my body started to complain at the thought of going out again – not least because I hadn't had any food. But, being a good bloke, I decided to chop along to the Bible study with my wife.

Nothing immediately spectacular happened as a result, but I did leave feeling glad that I'd made the effort. Something spectacular *does* happen over the long term, you see, when you spend time studying the Word of God with other believers. It's hard to explain but there are tangible benefits from regularly praying and studying the Bible with others. It kind of feeds your soul.

I am still often shocked at how few men go to home groups or are part of prayer triplets and so on. I think it's an absolute must for us blokes. So, make the effort: meet with other believers, devote yourself to the Word and reap the long-term benefits. On this particular occasion, it gave me an excuse to get some food from the chippie on the way home. Result!

Prayer: Give me a growing desire to meet with others to study Your Word and get to grips with prayer. Put people in my life who will journey with me. Amen.

30/Give what you've got

'All the believers were together and had everything in common.' **Acts 2:44**

Here's a cheeky bit of Greek for you. In the New Testament, the word for the way the early Christians lived is *koinonia*. It refers to the 'common' life they shared. No one claimed any possessions as their own, and as a result none of them went without. They lived together and shared all they had – it was the foundation of a really radical community.

It's a challenge when we read this bit of Acts to work out how we should live this out today. For myself, Karen and I have opened up our home and had people to stay with us long-term, even when we had small babies in the house. We've given cars away (yes, more than one), and sometimes given away the last bit of money we had, to help someone who was in a very tight spot. I don't say all this to point out how amazing we are, because we're not and anything good we've done is only because of the One who works on our characters, who has taken us on a rather steep learning curve! The reason I say it is because, although we have tried to make some radical choices and at times have emptied our accounts, we are still standing and doing just fine.

Do we trust God or not? Let's practise generosity and open up our lives and our wallets.

Prayer: Make me a generous man. Help me to open up my life and my wallet to help those who need a leg up. Amen.

31/ It's not a wake

'Every day they continued to meet together in the temple courts. They broke bread in their homes and ate together with glad and sincere hearts.' **Acts 2:46**

Sometimes when I take Communion in a church, it can feel more like a funeral than a celebration of the man who defeated death and saved my soul! I'm just being honest with you here. I know there is a sense of awe surrounding Communion and I know that reverence and respect are important. However, I think it's also important to express a bit of gratitude and joy (or, as the Bible calls it, here, 'glad[ness]').

So often I wonder if the fact we know Jesus should show more in our faces as well as our actions. The Early Church lived in community and 'did life' together because they had been touched by Him. I wonder sometimes if the stuff we get worked up about in church only shows that we've forgotten that a man died for us. Surely, if we kept that central message in our hearts and at the front of our minds we would behave differently? For me, it means that every so often I have to remind myself of the day I first met Jesus and think through the effect it had on me at the time. I reckon it's good to think back like that as it keeps your faith fresh.

Next time you take Communion, pause for a moment and think back. And then eat and drink with a smile on your face.

Prayer: Help me to have an overarching sense of joy rather than a pervading grumpiness. Help me to be a man who celebrates my faith. Amen.

32/Who's the man?

'For by the grace given me I say to every one of you: do not think of yourself more highly than you ought, but rather think of yourself with sober judgment, in accordance with the faith God has distributed to each of you.' **Romans 12:3**

There's an awesome scene in the film *Hotshots*, the comedy in which the antihero is unceremoniously dumped by the woman he loves. When people ask if he's all right, he gives this knockdown reply: 'It's OK, I've still got me!' In other words, the ego has landed!

It's amazing how many men suffer from this disease. Meet a bloke for the first time and often within a few minutes he's told you what he does for a living and how many talents and skills he's got. The Bible is clear that we need to get real about ourselves. My mate has a great way of putting it. He would say if anyone looks up to you or stands in admiration of anything you're doing, a brilliant response is: 'Listen, fella, if there's anything good you see in me, it's only because of the One who is greater than me who's changed my life.' It's a killer reply and puts all the focus on Jesus.

I think our job is to point beyond ourselves to Him, so this is a great way of doing that while also keeping our egos in check. Just a word of caution: don't start going around saying you've got a great gift of humility!

Prayer: Give me a humble heart and a grace that enables me to point beyond myself to Jesus. Amen.

Humility is not thinking less of yourself, it's thinking of yourself less.
C. S. LEWIS

33/Jigsaw

'We have different gifts, according to the grace given to each of us. If your gift is prophesying, then prophesy in accordance with your faith.' **Romans 12:6**

One of the best lessons we can learn is that any one of us has only a part of the jigsaw. None of us can do it all or we wouldn't need each other. The problem is that in the Hollywood version of masculinity the hero is often the man who *can* do it all. He can take on a whole army and still be an awesome dad with a tender heart. It's rubbish. We need each other, and the guys who get that, and who understand their need to work with others, are the ones who truly succeed. In all honesty, it's my strong belief that God made it that way. Community and collaboration are in His very nature – I mean, look at the Trinity for a start!

The next lesson we need to learn is that people with different gifts from us will almost certainly have different insights from us. So, we need the grace to work with, not against, those who see things differently from us. (Of course, it's only fair to say that they may need a degree of grace themselves when dealing with *us*!) It's so easy to get this wrong, but totally awesome when we practise grace and get it right. Remember, you have got only part of the jigsaw. There is something that only you can bring to the table, and the same goes for those around you. So, pull together and crack on!

Prayer: Make me a team man, who works well with others and recognises all the different gifts they bring to the table. Amen.

34/Cheers

'If it is to encourage, then give encouragement; if it is giving, then give generously; if it is to lead, do it diligently; if it is to show mercy, do it cheerfully.' **Romans 12:8**

It's only recently that I've truly realised the power of cheering someone on. It's so easy to take people for granted and we let the days roll past and never find the time to encourage them in what they're doing. Yet it's such a simple thing to do, and for those on the receiving end it can be really transforming. So, take the time to notice what people are doing and then take some more time to say a few words that will build them up and spur them on.

Not only will it make a huge difference to them but also it will do something to your heart and soul. The times I have cheered on my mates or my family have been some of my happiest moments – partly, I believe, because it has been a completely selfless act. Many of the things we do, if we're honest, we do with one eye to our own advantage; but when we cheer someone on with no thought of ourselves, it is one of the most unselfcentred things we can do.

Now, some people have a true gift of encouragement and it comes easily to them. In all honesty, I don't. It's something I have to work at – and so I do. So, how about you? When was the last time you showed appreciation to people around you or congratulated someone on doing something well, even if it wasn't directly connected with you? Go on, give it a go and see how you feel. As it happens, it will make you the kind of bloke other people want to spend time with – but don't do it for that reason, do it because it is right!

Prayer: May I get a reputation for being generous with praise, a man who always cheers other people on. Amen.

35/Stay on track

'Be strong and very courageous.
Be careful to obey all the law my
servant Moses gave you; do not
turn from it to the right or to the
left, that you may be successful
wherever you go.' **Joshua 1:7**

Joshua is about to steam into the promised
land. He's got to lead the fighting men across
the Jordan while it's in flood and go to war in a
country they once hadn't wanted to enter for
fear of giants (Num. 13:31-33). Years have gone
by since then, however, and Joshua now has his
invasion orders and they are preparing to fight
their way in.

There's a significant promise attached to these
orders as well. Joshua is told that no one will
be able to stand against him and that God will
never leave him or forsake him (Josh. 1:5). Nice
one! However, read verse 7 and there's a kind of
condition attached to the promise: Be careful to
obey the law of Moses and don't stray to the right

or the left. The implication is obvious. If Joshua fails to keep this condition, he will be stepping outside God's protection and blessing.

It's a sharp reminder to us guys who call on God to be with us and help us. Are we fulfilling our side of the deal and living biblically-informed kingdom lives? It's not rocket science, and this is not a deep thought. It is, however, a question worth asking yourself today: Am I straying to the right or the left or am I bang on track?

Prayer: Examine my life, Lord, and keep me true to Your will and obedient to Your Word. Prompt me whenever I begin to stray. Amen.

36/It's not about yoga

'Keep this Book of the Law always on your lips; meditate on it day and night, so that you may be careful to do everything written in it. Then you will be prosperous and successful.' **Joshua 1:8**

Usually when people talk about meditation, we immediately think of yoga, kung-fu monks or hippies sitting under a tree looking a bit spaced out. I asked the guys in the office what was the first thing the word brought to mind and they said it was someone sitting cross-legged in the lotus position, humming. Interesting ...

What I'm into is pondering and contemplating. I get a verse from the Bible and I roll it around my mind and reflect on it. I generally sit on the edge of a chair with my hands on my knees and think about God and what the verse is saying to me. I soak it up and try to commit it to memory and make it a part of me. It's an awesome discipline

– and it also tends to make me feel quite chilled out, which is a bonus!

Give it a go. If you make it a regular feature of your life to take time to ponder some scripture and contemplate your faith, you'll reap the benefit. That is, after all, the promise of the second part of this verse – you will be prosperous and successful if you do this! Us blokes are by nature often activists, but let's take the time out that we need to take.

Prayer: As I meditate and ponder on Your Word, bring me into a deeper understanding of You, Your power and Your plan for my life. Amen.

37/Man up!

'Have I not commanded you? Be strong and courageous. Do not be afraid; do not be discouraged, for the LORD your God will be with you wherever you go.' **Joshua 1:9**

Three times in this passage God tells Joshua to be strong and courageous. I reckon that when He keeps saying something, it's for a very good reason. In this case, it's because Joshua is about to go to war and it's going to be brutal, relentless and long-drawn-out. He's got to take down whole armies and cities to establish the people of Israel in their new land. So, no wonder God keeps drumming the message home!

It's a good verse for us guys to take on board as well. I don't know what you're up against today, or this week. I don't know what trials and tests are coming your way, and perhaps you don't either. What I do know, though, is that God stands for those who love Him and He doesn't let us go through more than we can bear. The truth is that no matter what confronts us, those of us who are in Christ can face up to the challenge and tough it out because God will be with us wherever we go.

Keep that truth up your sleeve and remind yourself of it when the pressure is really on!

Prayer: Thank You, God, that wherever I go and whatever I face, You are right there with me. Help me always to be strong and courageous. Amen.

38/Get on with it

> 'So Joshua ordered the officers of the people: "Go through the camp and tell the people, 'Get your provisions ready. Three days from now you will cross the Jordan here to go in and take possession of the land the LORD your God is giving you for your own.'" ... Then they answered Joshua, "Whatever you have commanded us we will do, and wherever you send us we will go."'
>
> **Joshua 1:10-11,16**

Joshua gives the order and the men get ready to move out. There seems to be no questioning, no hesitation and no delay. This is radical obedience ahead of a season of war and conquest. It's stirring stuff!

When I gave my life to Jesus and I realised that He was now my Commanding Officer, I felt like these guys obeying Joshua. I sat on the edge of my bed and said something like: 'I will go wherever You tell me to go and do whatever You ask me to do, no matter what.' I was gripped by the truth of who Jesus was. After all, I reasoned that as God was real and He had created the universe, no other response was possible.

I think this is an understanding of following Jesus that we need to keep coming back to. The danger is that over the years we can lose our sense of what it means to be radically obedient to Him and we start to make conditions and somehow lose our edge. Let's instead stay sharp, focused, obedient and ready to get stuck in when God gives the order!

Prayer: I commit to submitting to You as my Commanding Officer. I will live my life in readiness to obey Your orders. Amen.

39/Foot in

'"Now then, choose twelve men from the tribes of Israel, one from each tribe. And as soon as the priests who carry the ark of the LORD – the Lord of all the earth – set foot in the Jordan, its waters flowing downstream will be cut off and stand up in a heap." So when the people broke camp to cross the Jordan, the priests carrying the ark of the covenant went ahead of them.' **Joshua 3:12-14**

When Moses led the Israelites across the Red Sea, the waters parted before they even got their feet wet. What they did was still a mind-blowing act of faith, don't get me wrong – but the negotiation of the River Jordan described here takes it to a different level. In this case, the priests actually had to go and step into a river that was in flood.

Sometimes we need to step out in faith *before* we see God intervene. We may have heard Him speak to us, telling us to go in a particular direction, but that doesn't mean He will line everything up for us and make it easy. The fact is that often we need to exercise trust in Him and put our feet into flood waters. We've experienced this at CVM, the ministry I lead, many times. We've known that God wanted us to go in a certain direction but haven't yet got in place everything we needed to make it happen. In some cases, there has been a serious lack of money or staff. It has been our version of a river in flood and it's been scary to just step into it anyway. But when God has spoken, and you're sure of it, you can be confident you won't be swept away.

Prayer: When the time comes for me to step into the flood waters, give me the guts to exercise faith and put my trust in You. Amen.

[AN IDIOT'S GUIDE]

40/Adultery

'But the man who commits adultery is an utter fool, for he destroys himself.' **Proverbs 6:32 (NLT)**

I read an interview with Bradley Wiggins in the paper, at the time when it seemed more and more likely that he was going to win the 2012 Tour de France – the first Brit to win the race since it started in 1903. Asked if he'd taken performance-enhancing drugs, he said something like: 'Why would I? I'd risk losing everything!'

Now he's won the Tour, it's estimated that he stands to gain £5 million from endorsements in the first year alone, and one paper put his potential earnings at £20 million. Plus, he's a national hero with a knighthood, and a reputation for sportsmanship because of his unselfish behaviour towards his rival Cadel Evans and his teammate Mark Cavendish during the race. The French are calling him 'Le Gentleman'. All that would go out of the window if he tested positive.

He'd become a pariah. He'd be a complete idiot – 'an utter fool' – to risk that.

If I commit adultery, I stand to lose everything – my wife, my reputation, my kids' trust in me and in people in general. But, much more important, as a follower of Jesus I'd damage His reputation in the eyes of sceptics. I might well discourage other disciples. Why would I risk all that? I'd be a complete idiot.

If you're about to do it, or fantasising about doing it, you should stop and think about idiots. The same is true, for that matter, if you're single and are thinking of having sex outside of marriage. But suppose you've already done it? What's been destroyed may never be fully restored, but there *is* a way back for idiots, through Jesus. Fortunately, He specialises in idiots, and died for them!

**Prayer: Lord, in my weakness
please keep me from
being an idiot and falling
into adultery. Amen.**

41/Comfort zone

'But God said to him, "You fool! You will die this very night. Then who will get everything you worked for?" Yes, a person is a fool to store up earthly wealth but not have a rich relationship with God.'

Luke 12:20-21 (NLT)

This comes at the end of Jesus' story about the 'rich fool'. Imagine someone calling you an idiot - not 'a bit of a lad', or a daredevil who does outrageous stuff, but someone who's just really stupid. Someone who's missed out on something fantastic and ended up with rubbish. Someone who's a loser forever, who's done themselves terrible damage. It's not a question of deserving sympathy instead of 'Idiot!', because that isn't an insult, it's just the truth. You knew deep down what you should have done but you took the easy way out through apathy, stubbornness, selfishness, fear - whatever.

Imagine that this person is someone you really respect. They had your best interest at heart but you ignored them. You can't argue the toss – they're right, you're the worst kind of idiot and that's all there is to it.

Imagine that it's unbelievably worse than that, because the one who is calling you an idiot is God.

Why is the man in the story in this nightmare position? Because he did what I'm naturally inclined to do – what most of us do, or would if we had the money: he used his wealth to build a comfort zone. The power and love of Jesus should be our comfort zone, and in them we should be out there fighting His battle in the uncomfortable world. Our money should be one of our weapons. God help me, I don't want to be an idiot!

Prayer: Lord, I won't like it but please keep kicking me out of my idiotic comfort zone and show me how to use my money for You. Amen.

42/Just do it

'But everyone who hears these words of mine and does not put them into practice is like a foolish man who built his house on sand. The rain came down, the streams rose, and the winds blew and beat against that house, and it fell with a great crash.' **Matthew 7:26-27**

'We need to be "steeped in the Word" ... ' *And then just do it.*

'We're a Spirit-and-Word church in our Sunday services – and sometimes even signs-and-wonders.' *And what about works? Just do it – outside on Mondays.*

'Our church leader has an amazing grasp of doctrine. He's able to show that the Word satisfies at all intellectual levels.' *Yeah, but just do it – if only the bits that are easy to understand. It wasn't meant to be rocket science. The developing world* is full of 'heroes of the faith' who haven't got a whole Bible or can't even read.

'We're so thankful for the teaching we get in our church.' *Great! So, now you can just do it, yeah?*

'It's no good expecting people to evangelise until they are confident of the doctrinal basis of their faith and are able to answer objections.' *Learn on the job – it's the best way. Just do it!*

'That was an amazing sermon this week.' *Thanks. So, now just do it. Some of it. Any of it.*

'I love the Word. I've memorised 100 Bible verses!' *Fantastic, but … Oh! Is that the sound of rushing water? How well do idiots float?*

Prayer: Lord, melt my heart with Your Word and help me not just to study it but to *do* it. Amen.

43/Speak up

'Only fools say in their hearts,
"There is no God."' **Psalm 14:1 (NLT)**

On telly and in films, committed Christians are
often seen at worst as brainwashed victims of
a cult and at best as comic figures, naive and
irrelevant to real life. We're idiots or worse. Which
can stealthily erode our confidence and gradually
close our mouths. And a 'faith' is seen as
something that – if you must – you can consider
coolly and impartially, weighing up the evidence
to decide whether to give it a go or not. Take it or
leave it, it's up to you.

But the Bible says different. There's no impartial
ground. Deep down, everyone knows about
God and if they reject Him, the Bible calls *them*
idiots. That seems harsh – it's certainly suicidally
bigoted by today's standards. Unless ... it really *is*
something of the truth that they know deep down
but still reject. How could there be any other
word than 'idiot' for someone who does that? But
they don't deserve our ridicule – it's not that sort

of 'Idiot!'. It's tragic and it's deadly serious – not an insult but a fact. I was just a hopeless idiot myself until I was rescued by Jesus, and I need Him every day to stop me lapsing back into being one again.

We need to explain the truth humbly to those who seem to be rejecting it. And when we do it, in the face of our powerful, scornful culture, we have to have confidence in the gospel. It's the power of God for rescuing people. In this case, it's not us who are the idiots!

Prayer: Lord, I'm not a fool. Please give me the confidence to speak up about You. Amen.

44/Mouthing off

'The tongue also is a fire, a world of evil among the parts of the body. It corrupts the whole body, sets the whole course of one's life on fire, and is itself set on fire by hell.'

James 3:6

The proverb 'Sticks and stones may break my bones, but words will never hurt me' is the biggest pile of rubbish ever written. Of course words hurt - they can cut really deeply into our hearts and minds. I've met blokes who had negative things said to them by parents, teachers or mates when they were kids and it's still having a massive impact on their lives 30 or 40 years later. The tongue has amazing powers of destruction. And that's why James writes this here.

It's not only that, though. The implication of this passage is that the words we say also have the power to corrupt us, too. If you think about it, there's a huge amount of truth in this. If all that comes out of your mouth is bitterness and complaint, chances are you will end up a very bitter and complaining person. That's just the way it is.

The bottom line is this: the best thing you can do is to get a grip on your mouth. If you've got nothing good to say, don't say anything. Ask God to help you to keep your tongue under control and exercise some discipline along the way.

Prayer: Lord, I pray that today, no matter how much stress I'm under, You will help me to keep a grip on your mouth. Amen.

Fire and swords are slow engines of destruction, compared to the tongue of a gossip.
RICHARD STEELE

45/Forked tongue

'With the tongue we praise our Lord and Father, and with it we curse human beings, who have been made in God's likeness.' **James 3:9**

It's the weirdest thing, really, but we have a tremendous ability to wear masks and live very hypocritically. I'm guilty of this myself. It's Sunday and you're getting ready for church and everyone is running late. Tensions rise and though you try to keep a lid on it, you fail and say something you then wish you hadn't said. Fifteen minutes later and you're in church suffering an action song and then getting stuck into some intercessory prayer. It's a nightmare. One minute you're all angry and hot under the collar and then a short while later you're Mr Butter-wouldn't-melt in a church meeting.

It's not just in church that this happens, of course – it can happen anywhere. We can be all godly in one scenario and yet being hugely unkind with our words in another context minutes later. Once, a waiter in a restaurant over the road from a Christian conference told me he could always tell when Christians were in because they moaned more than most other people. How gutting is that? So, let's be consistently kind and generous with our words – not just in church but wherever we find ourselves.

Prayer: Help me always to be kind with my words. Don't let me be a man who talks one way in one place but quite another way somewhere else. Amen.

46/Wise?

'Who is wise and understanding among you? Let them show it by their good life, by deeds done in the humility that comes from wisdom.'
James 3:13

Blokes are experts at everything and that's a fact and my expert opinion. We've usually got a definitive answer to every question under the sun. I've met a lot of guys in church who have an opinion on every single aspect of the church's life and mission. Sometimes these men wonder why they aren't elders or leaders.

I think this verse gives us a good insight into why they aren't. The wise among us are known not just by the opinions they have but also by the way they conduct their lives. They serve quietly in the shadows and don't push themselves forward. They are at peace with the world: they believe the best of other people and give them the benefit of the doubt, and rarely get into long-drawn-out disputes. Why? Because they listen first before they spout off. Those people who listen first do so because they humbly believe that other people, too, have something to contribute. They believe the best of others because they've taken time to get to know people and go beyond the first impressions we all tend to form.

These are the kind of people we need to strive to become like.

Prayer: I don't want to be a man who shoots his mouth off ignorantly. Give me the wisdom to be humble, to listen and think before speaking. Amen.

47/Do your bit

'Whoever oppresses the poor shows contempt for their Maker, but whoever is kind to the needy honours God.' **Proverbs 14:31**

I'll keep this brief and to the point. I've had the privilege of travelling a fair bit to various places around the world and in the course of my travels I've seen a huge amount of poverty. I've eaten with people living in slum houses and I've wept with someone dying in a cramped shack made of rubbish, who couldn't get to hospital. I could go on.

Our lives are often consumed by 'rich world' problems. We get frustrated when our train is late or our favourite brand of something or other is not available in the supermarket. Let's get real! I don't think we can ignore the developing world – or the needs of the poor in our own backyard. All I ask today is that you think seriously about your own response. Could you sponsor a child? Could you support some project financially? Could you take some leave and offer your skills to a charity?

Could you share Christmas with someone who is on their own or give up your holiday to work in a homeless shelter?

I just think we need to take this proverb seriously. After all, to care for those in need is to honour God!

_____

Prayer: Show me how I can use my resources to help those in need. Help me to be a man who doesn't just walk on by but does his bit. Amen.

_____

48/Take it on board

'Mockers resent correction, so they avoid the wise.' **Proverbs 15:12**

Let's be honest, no one really likes getting criticism. It's tough to take it on the chin, especially when you've poured a lot of time and energy into something. I reckon, though, that if you spend your life avoiding criticism, you're going to end up making some pretty daft decisions. As painful as it can be to hear it, getting feedback is one of the best things we can do.

My advice is to surround yourself with people who are wiser and more clear-sighted than you, more gifted than you, more able than you but who love you and are on your side. If you do that, you will protect yourself from falling into all kinds of errors that could have been easily avoided. Some of my closest friends are my closest friends precisely because they have cared enough to write to me, phone me or take me aside when they've thought I was making a mistake. They haven't always been right, mind you – but that's not the point. The fact is that even if such friends are wrong a hundred times, the one time they hit the nail on the head and save you from a nightmare – or just from doing something less well than you might have done – makes up for the hundred other times!

So, learn to get feedback and seek advice. Sometimes it can be a game-changer.

Prayer: Surround me with people who are wise and clear-sighted and help me to take their advice. Guard me from being arrogant and falling into error. Amen.

49/Under the mattress

'Do not store up for yourselves treasures on earth, where moths and vermin destroy, and where thieves break in and steal.'
Matthew 6:19

That was the old way, wasn't it? Stuff a pile of banknotes under the mattress for a rainy day. Many of us have had it drilled into us from an early age that it's good and right to save and plan for the future. I'm not going to knock that, but I do want to think about it. At what point does saving for a rainy day become toxic?

I think it does so when it becomes an obsession. I've met guys who panic when the amount in their bank account drops below a figure that (as it happens) is way more than I earn in a year. Crazy! Or there's that preoccupation with having the latest iGadget. I know others who are obsessed with upscaling their cars and houses and everything they have and get addicted to online estate agents and so on. They end up spending most of their lives dreaming of something better, bigger or flasher.

Jesus simply tells us not to go there. It's all temporary – you can't take any of it with you. My view is this: Keep your life lean and stripped back. Enjoy nice things but don't let them become your master or your driver. Here's a tip: if you find yourself really wanting some piece of kit, don't just go out and buy it. Park the idea for a couple of days. If the desire leaves you, bless someone else instead with an act of generosity. That's a kingdom way forward.

Prayer: Keep my eyes fixed on what really matters and guard me from wasting my energy, time and money chasing what is essentially temporary. Amen.

50/Changed lives

'But store up for yourselves treasures in heaven, where moths and vermin do not destroy, and where thieves do not break in and steal.' **Matthew 6:20**

So, what is your treasure in heaven? I guess there are loads of interpretations of what it might be, but let me tell you what grabs me in this. I think it's all about people. One day, we will die – that's a fact. We will die and we'll be with Jesus for eternity. I think that when that time comes, there will be reunions in heaven – with members of our family, colleagues from work, people we walked with, fell out with and then made up with, people we encountered quite randomly. I think there will be surprises, too, when we discover who will be sharing eternity with us.

And I think we will receive a reward according to what we did with the talents and opportunities God gave us; but I don't think it will relate to how nice we were to people (good though it is to be nice!). Rather, I think our reward – our 'treasure' – will relate to the people we led to Christ, or at least sowed a seed of faith in them. I think there will be conversations that go something like this: 'I'm here with you now because you prayed for me and you didn't give up on telling me about Jesus.'

That's a treasure that has an eternal value.

_____

Prayer: Help me to keep focused on things that have eternal value, so that one day there will be people in heaven with me because of my witness. Amen.

_____

51/ Head down or head up?

'For where your treasure is, there your heart will be also.' **Matthew 6:21**

Such a simple line, but so true!

What are you really passionate about? Your football team? Your family? Your work? Your motorbike? I guess that a way to find out is to be honest about what takes up most of your head space. Who or what dominates your thoughts when you average it out? Who or what gets most of your time and your wallet? The challenge for us as followers of Jesus is always to have a sense of our destiny – not in an intense way but more as a kind of subroutine constantly ticking away in the background. We need to keep our perspective on what life is really about. Then, when something begins to dominate our thoughts in an unhealthy way, we will naturally pull ourselves together.

I'll give you an example. I totally love motorbikes and have done ever since I can remember. I don't just like riding them, I like looking at them and reading about them. About four years ago, I realised that this was probably a bit of an obsession and was taking up too much head space for a Christian – so I sold my bike.

I've just dipped my toe back in the water and I now have a bike again which we are using for some filming work with CVM. It feels different this time, though, because my perspective has changed and it's not a big deal for me. I could let go of it whenever I wanted to – I think! And that's a lot healthier.

Perhaps you need to do the same with something you're losing perspective over. Where your treasure is, there your heart will be also. So, keep your treasure in heaven, not – say – your garage.

Prayer: Point out to me anything in my life that is becoming an unhealthy obsession. Help me to keep my heart focused on heavenly treasure, not junk. Amen.

52/The eyes have it

'The eye is the lamp of the body. If your eyes are healthy, your whole body will be full of light. But if your eyes are unhealthy, your whole body will be full of darkness. If then the light within you is darkness, how great is that darkness!'

Matthew 6:22-23

A quick word on the Greek first. The word translated 'healthy' here actually means (or, at least, implies) 'generous'. And the word 'unhealthy' implies 'stingy'.

In other words, if you look at the stuff you have and you're willing to be generous with it, you will be 'full of light'; but if you are mean, then you're heading into darkness. That's spot on. I know people who are basically stingy and, to be honest, they're not the kind of people you'd want to hang out with. Their tight-fistedness gets a bit tiresome, frankly. Not only that, I've found that people who are stingy are often also among the most covetous people I know: they lust after stuff – and women, too – with their eyes more than others. They're just unhealthy people.

On the other hand, the generous people I know are among the most grace-filled and fun-filled – you really want to be around them. Personally, I've felt for a long time that the more truly generous a person is, the more likely it is that the presence of Jesus has penetrated deeply into their lives. People who are generous with their cash also tend to be generous with their time, their help and their praise. In other words, this quality has filled their lives, as these verses imply that it will – either way!

Prayer: Make me a man known for being generous, not for being stingy. Make me generous with my money, my time, my help and my praise. Amen.

53/The bottom line

'No one can serve two masters. Either you will hate the one and love the other, or you will be devoted to the one and despise the other. You cannot serve both God and Money.' **Matthew 6:24**

Well, that's pretty blunt, and there's not much more to say, really. Basically, Jesus is telling us that we have a choice: either we serve Him or we serve money. It's up to us.

I don't think there is necessarily anything wrong with money in and of itself. If we didn't have it, we would only end up trading something else. The issue is: does your money serve you or do you serve it? As far as I'm concerned, our money is there to help us do certain things but we must never let it control us or become an obsession. Maybe you just don't have enough cash coming in – I've certainly been there and I know how it can fill your thoughts. That's not the kind of preoccupation Jesus is talking about here, however. This is about the *love* of money – or else a fear of not having enough that results in you not trusting God (which is why Jesus goes on to talk about anxiety a little later).

So, ask yourself today: Where do you put your trust? Who or what are you truly dependent on? Be honest about this. If it's not God, ask Him to help you sort your heart out with Him and work it through. Let's be clear about this: one day, when you're breathing your last, the size of your bank balance isn't going to mean very much to you personally, is it?

Prayer: I will trust You, God, with all my heart and strength and won't rely on my own resources. I will serve You and not make money my master. Amen.

54/Bigot

'Do not judge, or you too will be judged.' **Matthew 7:1**

We need to get some quick clarity on this verse, as it's often totally misused. Christians often quote it in defence of anyone who has stepped out of line in some way. Sentiments like 'Well, it's not our place to judge, is it?' get bandied about in total error. It's perfectly acceptable to judge on an issue of behaviour. For example, there is no way I would go to a church whose pastor believes in free love! I think we would all judge that to be just a bit out of order.

So, where does this verse kick in? For me, it's all about not having a hypercritical attitude. It's about not being the sort of bloke who likes to assess how holy (or otherwise) people are and sit in judgment on their personalities and gifts, their flaws and problems. It's one thing to arrive at a considered judgment on some issue but it's another thing entirely to be a self-righteous, opinionated plonker.

There's a great cure for this sort of attitude which I can really recommend. I'll explain it tomorrow. For now, though, let's wind our necks in and pray hard that we will see other people in a positive light and not look down on them, as those who like to sit in judgment tend to do. Essentially, people like that think they are better than everyone else. Sad, innit?

Prayer: Help me to see other people in a positive light. Guard my heart from a judgmental attitude and don't let me ever become a self-righteous fool. Amen.

55/You plank!

'Why do you look at the speck of sawdust in your brother's eye and pay no attention to the plank in your own eye?' **Matthew 7:3**

Basically, it's called having a blind spot. By definition, you don't know it's there because you can't see it. It takes someone else to point it out – unless you happen to get a sudden moment of clarity and realise for yourself how out of order you have been.

Here's an honest example. Once, I was making an observation about the way someone was behaving in meetings when one of my team said something like: 'You do realise you're a bit hard to get close to, don't you?' I was stunned. I had the impression I was an easygoing, cheerful sort of chap. 'What?' I said. 'Well,' they said, 'you've got a grumpy face and you're very focused and you're just not easy to get close to.' It was a total revelation to me! There was I waxing lyrical about someone else's character defect and I had no idea I had my own stuff to deal with. Thank God for close friends who point out your flaws!

So, here's my advice. Before you go around judging everyone else, make sure you haven't got a lump of four-by-two in your own eye. Let's ensure that our own lives are on track before we start going around being Mr I've-got-it-all-sorted.

Prayer: Point out to me today any planks in my own eye. Help me to remember that, like everyone, I have blind spots. Amen.

56/Loose the chains

'Is not this the kind of fasting I have chosen: to loose the chains of injustice … and break every yoke?'
Isaiah 58:6

So, there I was, standing in a slum in India. I'm surrounded by poverty and it's pretty grim. I'm in the home of a woman who has nothing except the one room she shares with five other people. One of them is her husband, who basically beats her up and the kids as well. It's not good and I feel powerless. It feels so wrong that any human being should have to live this way, deprived of even the most basic things she needs to be safe and secure. The fact that her husband earns one rupee a day and then throws it down his neck in booze, leaving his kids to go hungry, is an outrage.

So, how do we even begin to make a difference? I think the answer is that it's up to each and every one of us to work out our response. What I do know, however, is that there is a biblical mandate to take action. I believe strongly that if we ignore the developing world and the needs of the poor, we will anger God. There is loads you and I can do. We can raise money, sponsor children, use our talents and skills, give our time. All I suggest today is that you meditate on this verse and listen to what the Holy Spirit is asking of you.

Prayer: Stir me to action and show me how I can help to loose the chains of injustice. I know You want this of me. Amen.

Injustice anywhere is a threat to justice everywhere.
MARTIN LUTHER KING, JR.

57/ Do something!

'Is it not to share your food with the hungry and to provide the poor wanderer with shelter ...?' Isaiah 58:7

While I was travelling in the developing world, I had the privilege of visiting what is called a 'child survival programme'. Basically, pregnant women are taught how to keep their babies healthy and given free milk and vegetables to ensure that their little ones are born alive and survive their early years. Where these programmes have been put in place, the infant mortality rate has actually fallen to zero. Amazing! Supporting such projects is one way to respond to this verse.

But what about our own backyard? Do you take time to chat to the guy selling the *Big Issue*? How about buying him a coffee and a roll? Have you ever given time to a homeless shelter and hung out with the blokes there? I think there is a strong mandate for us to give our money, time and hearts to those in need, and there are needs on our doorsteps as well as thousands of miles away. I guess you could say that poverty in the rich West is very different to life in a slum in the developing world. Well, perhaps – but it's still poverty! Just think how horrific it must be to sleep on the streets on a winter's night in Britain. The fact that the poor will always be with us shouldn't stop us from getting stuck in.

So, how about it? What are you going to do?

Prayer: Give me Your heart for people, and especially for the poor. Give me the compassion to want to make a difference. Amen.

58/Boom time!

'Then your light will break forth like the dawn and your healing will quickly appear; then your righteousness will go before you, and the glory of the Lord will be your rear guard.' **Isaiah 58:8**

I find myself in lots of meetings where people are praying for revival and crying out for God to move powerfully around the world. Fair play, I get that. However, I'll give you a key to how to make it happen. If you pour out your life on behalf of the needy, you will see the power of God at work. I wonder if we see so little of this because we don't reflect His heart. Us blokes are shockers for just pulling up the drawbridge and getting on with our own lives and focusing entirely on our families and (sometimes) a few others. I believe, however, that there is a call for something more radical from us that so reflects the heart of God that we will see His power at work in a quite extraordinary way.

When I was in my mid twenties, I planted a church in a very tough place. I haven't got space to go into all the details here, but let's just say that I went almost overnight from having a very conservative view of the power of God to a completely different perspective. We saw profound answers to prayer: healings, conversions and divine breakthroughs in people's lives that blew our minds. It was a 'boom' moment. My wife and I opened our home and we poured out our lives to serve the needy. And in turn God poured out His love and power.

So, how about it, fella? You want to see God move? You want His glory to be your rear guard? Then get stuck in!

Prayer: Give me the guts and the tenacity to make a difference to broken people's lives. May Your glory be my rear guard. Amen.

59/Sow what?

'Do not be deceived: God cannot be mocked. A man reaps what he sows.' **Galatians 6:7**

Simple, this. You get back in bucketloads what you dish out to other people. If you're bitter, you will get back bitterness. Go through life with a smile and people will mostly smile back. Be a man of peace and peace will surround you. Lie and you'll fall foul of your own deception or the deceit of others. Be generous and people will be generous in return. Get the point? I could go on and on, but I'll spare you. I want to keep this brief.

I don't know where you are right now – on a train, in a car or perhaps on a plane, in the bath, kicking back in an armchair ... Stop right now and ask God how you are doing when it comes to this adventure called life. Specifically, ask Him now what you're sowing.

Then listen.

Then act.

Let's face it, it's so easy to walk past a need and do nothing. It's easy to keep our wallets in our pockets. It's easy to think that someone else will pick up the problem and so we don't have to. Sayings like 'Charity begins at home' give us an excuse to ignore the poor. Many people do live that way. But it's not the kind of life we are called to.

Prayer: Father, what am I sowing? Show me how I'm doing. Show me especially what I need to change and give me the guts to do it. Amen.

60/Dig in!

'Let us not become weary in doing good, for at the proper time we will reap a harvest if we do not give up.'
Galatians 6:9

Sometimes it takes time before you see the breakthrough you long for. Any vision you have, if it's from God, is worth fighting for, right? In my experience, when God gives you a heart for something, the result you want rarely gets delivered easily. It takes time and hard graft. This is especially true when it comes to loving people and doing good. So often it can feel like your kindness is being thrown back in your face and it's a totally thankless task.

Here's the deal, though. As we bring *Sowing/Growing/Knowing* in to land, let's remember that one of our jobs here on earth is to fight for what is right and to spend ourselves in doing good. We're men and we can take a hit, right? So, let's dig in and not quit at the first blow. So many guys get knocked out of the fight because of what are essentially superficial flesh wounds. Every time I have been tenacious and have done what God has called me to do, there has been a moment when it has all come together. I nearly quit planting a church once – it took me to my limits. After two years, though, we had seen many people become Christians and many lives changed. You never know what's around the corner!

Let me just say that I'm in the trenches with you on this kingdom adventure. It can be tough but it's worth it! So, let's crack on together and finish the fight.

Prayer: Strengthen my resolve and keep me strong and focused. Let me see a harvest of my family and my mates discovering Jesus and joining His kingdom. Amen.

More Bible notes for men written by Carl Beech.

Contains:

- 60 daily readings and prayers

- Two guest contributions

- Themes to encourage and challenge you

The Manual – Book 1:
Power/Poker/Pleasure/Pork Pies
ISBN: 978-1-85345-769-2
The Manual – Book 2:
Fighters/Keepers/Losers/Reapers
ISBN: 978-1-85345-770-8
The Manual – Book 3:
Son/See/Surf
ISBN: 978-1-85345-883-5
The Manual – Book 4:
Attitude/Gratitude/Proper Food
ISBN: 978-1-85345-886-6
The Manual – Book 5:
Shooting/Rooting/Booting
ISBN: 978-1-85345-941-2

Also available in eBook formats

For current prices visit www.cwr.org.uk/store
Available online or from Christian bookshops

Courses and seminars

Publishing and new media

Conference facilities

Transforming lives

CWR's vision is to enable people to experience personal transformation through applying God's Word to their lives and relationships.

Our Bible-based training and resources help people around the world to:
• Grow in their walk with God
• Understand and apply Scripture to their lives
• Resource themselves and their church
• Develop pastoral care and counselling skills
• Train for leadership
• Strengthen relationships, marriage and family life and much more.

Our insightful writers provide daily Bible-reading notes and other resources for all ages, and our experienced course designers and presenters have gained an international reputation for excellence and effectiveness.

CWR's Training and Conference Centres in Surrey and East Sussex, England, provide excellent facilities in idyllic settings – ideal for both learning and spiritual refreshment.

CWR Applying God's Word
to everyday life and relationships

CWR, Waverley Abbey House,
Waverley Lane, Farnham,
Surrey GU9 8EP, UK

Telephone: **+44 (0)1252 784700**
Email: **info@cwr.org.uk**
Website: **www.cwr.org.uk**

Registered Charity No 294387
Company Registration No 1990308

CVM
CHRISTIAN VISION FOR MEN

THE **code**
it's time for a new kind of man

connecting
men to Jesus
& the church to men

Partner with us
Connect a men's group
Start a men's group
Join a movement

Equipping and resourcing you to
share Jesus with the men around you

networking || events   resources || training

cvm.org.uk

CVM is a movement that offers a range of advice,
resources and men's events across the UK and beyond
The Hub, Unit 2, Dunston Rd, Chesterfield S41 8XA Tel: 01246 45248
Registered Charity in England & Wales (No.1071663)
A Company Ltd by Guarantee (No. 3623498)